The Successful Lawyer-Banker Relationship

A LawBiz® Management Special Report

by **Edward Poll**

Published by

LawBiz® Management Company
(a division of Edward Poll & Associates, Inc.)
421 Howland Canal
Venice, CA 90291
Phone: (800) 837-5880
Fax: (310) 578-1769
E-mail: EdPoll@LawBiz.com
Web site: www.LawBiz.com
Weblog: www.LawBizblog.com

Report design by Creative Quadrant, Inc.

Additional copies of this publication may be purchased from Edward
Poll & Associates, Inc., which also produces other publications of
interest to the legal and professional services communities. Discounts
are available for bulk orders.

Library of Congress Control Number: 2006908444

ISBN: 0-9654948-7-X

Table of Contents

Foreword

As a former airline CEO, I am well aware of how quickly competitive marketplace conditions change. For businesses to survive and thrive, it is imperative that their leadership teams be prepared for turbulent times. They must also be alert take advantage of business opportunities on short notice.

Law firms today are moving toward operating in a more businesslike fashion, rather than just as a group of professionals—and those that are truly businesslike will recognize that a key to responsible management is establishing a strong banking relationship. Importantly, banks are looking for profitable new niches, so law firms and banks are natural allies in today's competitive world.

Ed Poll's new report on the lawyer-banker relationship provides attorneys with straightforward information to understand the ins and outs of how to build a mutually beneficial relationship with one of the most important players in any business equation: your banker.

I know from firsthand experience how essential a strong banking relationship is to provide the necessary funds and financial services that allow a firm to maintain a strong foundation and maximize opportunities for growth. When you have the right relationship, a good banker will be creative in helping you become aware of opportunities to grow your business in ways you didn't know existed. The practical steps that Ed Poll provides in this little volume cover everything from how to choose a bank that's right for you, to how to improve your credit score and how to negotiate the best commercial loan to meet your needs. Throughout he explains what both sides should understand about and expect from each other in the lawyer-banker relationship.

This LawBiz® Special Report is a must-read if you want to take your law firm to a higher plateau.

—Howard Putnam
Former CEO of Southwest Airlines and Braniff Airlines

Speaker and Author of *The Winds of Turbulence: A CEO's Reflections on Surviving and Thriving on the Cutting Edge of Corporate Crisis*

Section 1:

Understanding the Lawyer-Banker Relationship

Introduction: The myths

Lawyers and law firms are generally attractive customers for banks. Banks value lawyers as being good financial prospects, with relatively low risk and good potential for providing new business referrals. Given these facts, lawyers should not be deterred from establishing banking relationships because of stereotypical myths. Let's begin our discussion by dispelling the common myths before embarking on discussing the steps involved in a solid lawyer-banker relationship.

Myth #1: Bankers only want to lend you money when you don't need it. The reality is that you first need to establish an ongoing relationship with a bank so that the bank understands your law firm's business dynamics and is comfortable with your ability to share risk in any loan or other transaction. Once an ongoing business relationship exists, you only have to pick up the phone and ask for a transfer of funds. In this scenario, the banker is pleased to do so because you already convinced him or her that you have a sound knowledge of your business

and profession. The banker understands that you understand what will be needed and when. Equally important, of course, the banker realizes that you understand when and how the loan or line of credit will be repaid.

Myth #2: Bankers hate surprises and will never honor an emergency need. Bankers are people, they want to help, and they will do so if approached in advance of a problem becoming a crisis. A good approach is to suggest alternative ways in which you might handle the particular challenge and ask for the banker's input and advice. A perfect example is disaster recovery. If you have established a good banking relationship, it's much easier to get an emergency loan to cover funds for rent, payroll, new supplies, new office arrangements, and other recovery needs if you review the situation in detail with your banker.

The reality: Mutual benefit

Banks and law firms are both professional services businesses and can develop mutually beneficial and effective business relationships if they work at them. The purpose of this special report is to provide any lawyer, but particularly those who have solo practices or small firms, with the framework to understand the following:

- How to choose a bank

- How bankers evaluate law firms as clients

- How to secure a loan

- How to use bank services that enhance law firm operations

- How to improve the banking relationship overall

Building a mutually beneficial and effective relationship with a bank is a critical step in making any law firm a more successful business. This LawBiz® Special Report provides the basics that will help you do just that.

> **"Money is like a sixth sense without which you cannot make a complete use of the other five."**
>
> —W. Somerset Maugham

Section 2:

Considering the Different Types of Banks*

Owing to the complexity of the U.S. banking system, choosing a bank requires some detailed thought. Compared to most other countries, the United States has traditionally had many more smaller and localized banks— reflecting such historical events as Andrew Jackson's disbanding of the Bank of the United States in the 1830s, establishment of the regionalized Federal Reserve System in 1913, and the banking laws passed during the 1930s to curb large bank abuses that supposedly contributed to the stock market crash. Until the 1990s, the only large national banks were investment banks like Goldman Sachs and Lehman Brothers (which underwrite securities offerings) and bank holding companies (shell organizations that raise capital in the financial markets to buy shares in existing banks).

---

* Information in this section was derived from the Web sites of the Federal Reserve Bank of Minneapolis (www.minneapolisfed.org), the Federal Deposit Insurance Corporation (www.fdic.gov), and the State of Connecticut Department of Banking (www.ct.gov/dob).

But that changed dramatically with the passage of the Gramm-Leach-Bliley Act in 1999, which greatly eased banking restrictions and allowed dramatic nationwide consolidation in banking. A major result is that the number of local financial institutions available for establishing a financial services relationship has shrunk by more than one-third since the mid-1990s.

Still, despite this ongoing change, the basic landscape of financial institutions available to serve law firms and lawyers continues to encompass the following three broad categories: commercial banks, thrifts, and credit unions. Note that generally, however, your choice should largely depend on convenience and personal relationships rather than institution type.

Commercial banks

These are banks in the most traditional sense. Commercial banks receive deposits and hold them in a variety of different accounts, extend credit through loans and other instruments, and facilitate the movement of funds. While commercial banks mostly specialize in short-term business credit, they also make consumer loans and mortgages and have a broad range of financial powers. Nationally chartered banks and community banks are both types of commercial banks.

> ► *National banks.* Commercial banks can elect to have a national charter, issued at the federal level, which subjects them to supervision by the Office of the Comptroller of the Currency (a division of the U.S. Treasury Department).

What Are Federal Reserve Banks?

Federal Reserve banks are the fiscal agents for the U.S. Treasury, which means that they are the federal government's bank. The Reserve banks offer many services to financial institutions, which makes them bankers' banks as well.

Reserve banks

- Hold the cash reserves of depository institutions and make loans to them

- Move currency and coin into and out of circulation, and collect and process millions of checks each day

- Provide checking accounts for the Treasury, issue and redeem government securities, and act in other ways as fiscal agent for the U.S. government

- Participate in the activity that is the primary responsibility of the Federal Reserve System, the setting of monetary policy

- **Supervise and examine commercial banks that are members of the Federal Reserve System for safety and soundness**

Source: Board of Governors of the Federal Reserve System

Or they can choose a state charter, which brings both federal and state supervision and regulation.

- *Community banks.* The community bank is a special category of the nationally chartered bank. They are small local banks that focus on small business loans and household deposits and loans. State-chartered banks that elect to join the Federal Reserve System are supervised by the Fed's Board of Governors (a responsibility delegated to the Federal Reserve district banks). The remaining state-chartered banks are supervised by both the state agency and the Federal Deposit Insurance Corporation (FDIC).

From a practical standpoint, most of these regulatory and organizational distinctions should not have any effect on the type of commercial bank you choose. The only exception is that state-chartered banks can choose not to join the Federal Reserve System. If it does choose to become a member of the Federal Reserve System, the state bank must obtain federal deposit insurance, which has for some years remained at $100,000 per depository account. The corollary is that deposits at some state banks may not be covered by FDIC insurance. The FDIC's Web site (www.fdic.gov) has a locator feature that lets you enter a bank's name and confirm whether or not deposits there are insured.

Thrifts

Thrifts, often still known by the term "savings and loan associations," are federally chartered to accept savings and small deposits and make loans primarily for real estate and construction purposes. Most of these institutions are technically owned by the depositors, who receive shares in the association in exchange for their deposits (which are insured by the FDIC in the same manner as deposits at commercial banks). Thrifts and their holding companies are

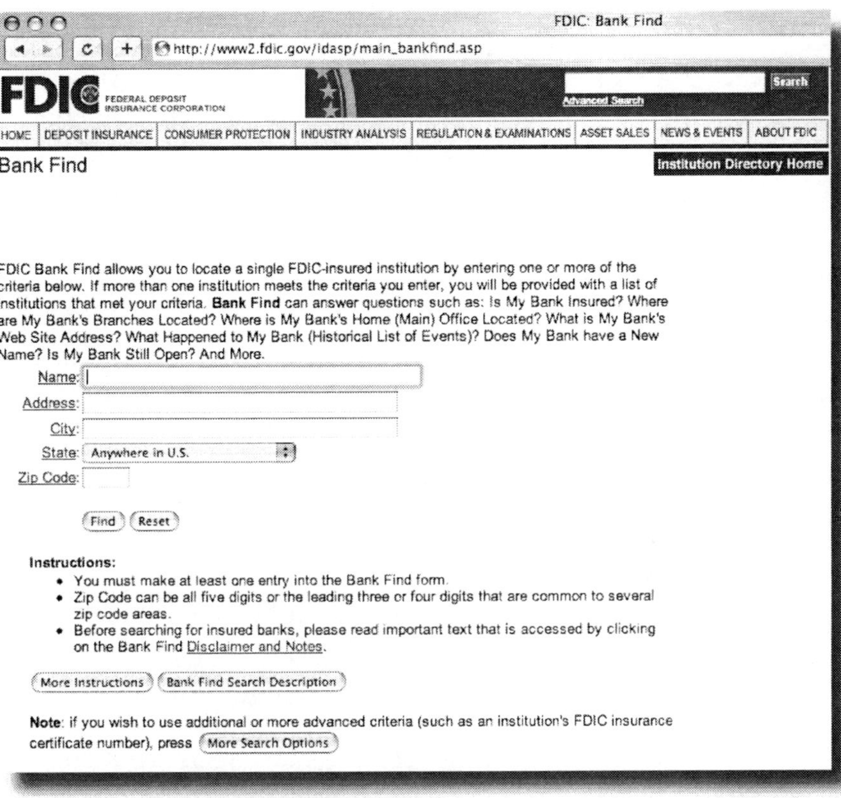

The FDIC's online Bank Find tool helps users identify FDIC-insured institutions.

supervised at the federal level by the Office of Thrift Supervision, a division of the Treasury Department.

Mutual savings banks, a close relative of thrifts, are state-chartered savings institutions that were originally designed to accept deposits from individuals and make residential mortgage loans. Over time, they have broadened the type of services offered and now are considered to be the functional equivalent of a commercial bank. Deposits at mutual savings banks are also insured by the FDIC, which acts as a supervisor along with state banking agencies.

The number of thrifts declined dramatically in the late 1980s and early 1990s. The savings and loan crisis of the 1980s forced many institutions to close or merge with others, at an extraordinary cost to the federal government. However, there has been a resurgence of interest in thrift ownership, which, thanks to the Gramm-Leach-Bliley Act, can now be an investment strategy for insurance companies and securities firms. To the average law firm, given the broadening of thrift services and the presence of FDIC insurance, the nature of thrift ownership should not be an issue.

Credit unions

Credit unions are not-for-profit financial cooperatives that initially required individuals to share a "common bond" for membership (such as employment at the same firm) in order to receive personal loans and other consumer banking services. Deregulation in the 1970s and 1980s gradually relaxed restrictions on both membership and the types of products and services offered by these financial institutions. Today, credit unions are largely indistinguishable from commercial banks, although they are exempt from federal and state taxes due to their not-for-profit status. Deposits at credit unions are termed "shares" and are insured by the federal government through a fund operated by the National Credit Union Administration, the federal agency also responsible for supervising national credit unions.

Credit unions accept deposits in a variety of accounts. All credit unions offer savings accounts, or time deposits. The larger institutions also offer checking and money market accounts. Credit unions' financial powers have expanded to include almost anything a bank or savings association can do, including making home loans, issuing credit cards, and even making some commercial loans. (Many lawyers use credit cards to finance growth. It may be expensive, but sometimes it is the only avenue open for the short term.)

Some commercial banks claim that the tax-exempt status of credit unions gives them a competitive advantage as far as the rates they can afford to pay on deposits and charge for loans. Credit unions are also localized and generally have a reputation of being very service-oriented institutions. However, they typically may not have the sophistication to accommodate such law firm needs as trust accounts and cash collection lockboxes.

Section 3:

Choosing Your Bank and Banker

Factors to consider

Not every lawyer can properly represent every client. Likewise and just as logically, not every bank is appropriate for every lawyer.

You should look for a bank that will give you the types of services you need and the level of responsiveness you want. An appropriate bank should be able to handle the needs of your firm as well as your personal banking needs. In addition, it should offer geographic convenience and have a solid reputation in the community. But it is also important to remember that large size does not always equate to impressive service or performance. (See Section 13 of this LawBiz® Special Report for the less-than-stellar experiences that some solo practitioners and small firms have had with several of the nation's largest banks.)

In picking a bank, understand the niches in which it specializes—for example, high-wealth individuals, large commercial accounts, small or midsize businesses and so forth. Consider whether the institution is locally or regionally owned, or whether it is an acquisition of a large national bank. Get suggestions or recommendations from your accountant, local bar association, and even other lawyers who you do not consider to be direct competitors. And don't shy away from banks that seem to emphasize doing business with other lawyers. The more a bank understands your business dynamics, the more helpful it can be. Plus, only banks that were grossly unethical would reveal any sensitive information about your law practice.

The primary contact

In considering your options, keep in mind that you should be forming a relationship with both a bank and a banker. There are, however, practical pluses and minuses to relying on just one primary banking contact in this era of bank consolidation, when changes in personnel can occur quickly. You do not want to rely extensively on one person who may suddenly leave. Just as a lawyer needs to have deep and wide relationships with clients' organizations, you want a range of contacts within your bank. Don't just limit yourself to dealing with only your loan officer or branch manager. Getting to know a senior manager, a vice president, or even the president of the bank will help you in the long run.

This is particularly true if the bank is involved in a merger. Your contacts could not tell you about a merger beforehand because of privacy restrictions. However, once you've established senior relationships, you can prepare for a pending merger by asking to be on the short list for early notification. If a merger does occur, ask to be introduced to the new people as soon as possible. If your bank is doing the acquiring, it puts you in a good position with a stronger bank that has new referral sources. Alternatively, if your bank is being acquired, you have to know who the new players are.

Your relationship goal

To contextualize the lawyer-banker relationship and what you want to obtain from it, think of the bank as a supplier. Suppliers provide lawyers with goods and services that, in turn, allow the law firm to deliver quality legal services to its clients. One of the essential suppliers, for any lawyer, is a reliable and helpful bank. Good banking relationships provide the necessary funds and financial services that allow a firm not only to maintain itself, but also to grow with the future. And, in addition to their inventory of money and trust services, bankers can be good referral sources for new business for lawyers.

Number of FDIC-Insured Institutions

1990 – 2006

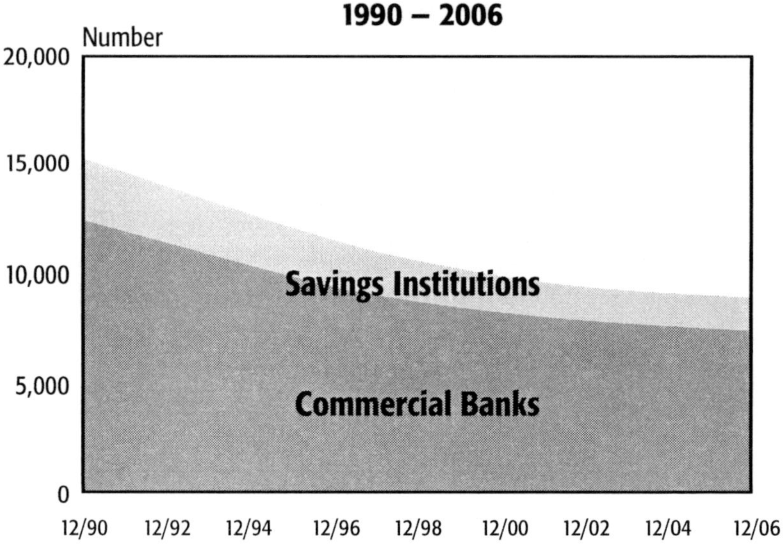

Number of FDIC-Insured Institutions By Asset Size

June 30, 2006

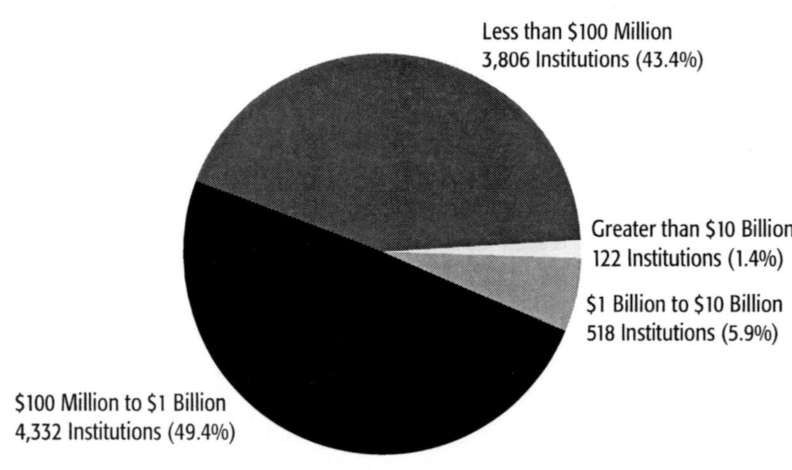

Section 4:

Demonstrating Your Business Sense

Bankers, as a matter of course, view and understand any law firm as a business, an entity with cash flow, receivables, revenues, and profits. Therefore, to build up a relationship of trust, lawyers need to educate their bankers, openly and candidly, on how their business operates. It should go without saying that lawyers need to understand their own business operation (often better than they do) and how it centers on the following key aspects that bankers inevitably review.

Business documentation

Your banker will need assurance that your firm is a viable, ongoing business. Accordingly, fundamental documentation of that fact should be collected and presented to the bank at the start of any new banking relationship. Key elements include the following:

- ▶ Partnership agreement or entity papers (corporate charter or LLP articles)

- ▶ Fiscal year-end financial statements for two to five years, prepared by an accountant

- ▸ Accounts receivable schedule

- ▸ Law firm tax returns for two to five years

- ▸ Personal financial statements and tax returns of the law firm's principals

- ▸ Evidence of business liability and malpractice insurance

The business plan

Most lawyers begin to realize that they are in trouble only after the money ceases coming in the door. However, cash flow cessation is usually the last symptom of a downward spiral that started long before. The point when cash stops coming in the door is much too late to start wondering if there is a problem. The seeds of the problem were undoubtedly sown weeks, months, or even years earlier. To foresee and thus avoid potential trouble down the road, lawyers need to plan the business side of their operations.

Planning for cash flow is very important to provide comfort to a banker when the bank is asked to make a loan. Accordingly, bankers normally request a business plan to facilitate any loan. Even if you have "challenges" in your business, you will need to address them in a business plan.

While the business plan does not need to be complex, it should be developed as the result of an organized process that includes these steps:

- ▸ Preparing the plan and getting agreement (or buy-in) from all key players in the firm. This

requires gathering historical information about financial performance, analyzing it, and drawing inferences about future performance.

► Identifying goals in terms of desired clients and new business.

► Creating a marketing plan.

► Creating a financial plan.

► Evaluating and revising the plan against ongoing performance.

Keep Accounts Receivable Reports at the Ready

Lawyers need to have a copy of their most recent accounts receivable aging report on their desks at all times. This report should clearly show which clients are up to date with their bills and which have fallen behind.

When a client calls to ask you to take on more work, look at the report. If the client has not paid in accord with his or her agreement and is past due on the account, you take a significant risk of increased unpaid billings by accepting more work from this client.

At this stage, the only financially responsible approach is to tell the client that you cannot take on any new matters until the bill for previous legal services is paid in full.

The receivables plan

Successful management of receivables is essential for law practices of every size. Banks understand this well. Yet it is a hard lesson for lawyers to grasp because they think that financial success means ever-rising billable hours. The truth is that a lawyer's inventory is *not* billable hours—it is the cash those hours represent. Bankers will expect that any lawyer will make sure clients know that they must pay their bills within 60 to 90 days.

Developing an effective receivables plan means taking

a businesslike approach to collecting money through a
process that includes the following:

- ▸ A written engagement letter that sets forth
  clients' obligations and responsibilities in paying
  their bills.

- ▸ A budget for events, time, and money so that
  clients both buy into and accept the budget and
  will not be surprised by what is billed.

- ▸ Accurate and prompt timekeeping records of
  all work done for clients, which will eliminate
  the estimated 10 to 15 percent revenue loss that
  otherwise might result when contemporaneous
  time entries are not made.

- ▸ Eliminating (not charging for) ancillary,
  overhead expenses such as photocopying to
  prevent extraneous reasons for slow payment.
  When such expenses are large, they should be
  outsourced and, if possible, billed directly to the
  client without a surcharge.

- ▸ Billing statements that are easy to understand
  and that clearly correlate actions taken on the
  client's behalf to the value realized by the client.

- ▸ Constant communications to make sure an
  actual or perceived problem neither exists nor
  results in a client deciding not to pay a bill.

- ▸ Use of a staff member, or collection service
  if necessary, to contact clients with overdue
  balances to request payment.

The marketing plan

Bankers know that new clients are the lifeblood of any business and that a scattershot marketing approach is counterproductive to securing new clients. It's far more effective to develop—and adhere to—a well thought-out marketing plan that consistently evaluates your tactics.

The best way to create a marketing plan is to define your specific marketing tactics, the hypothetical client targets they're aimed at, and the work those clients can or may give you. Here is an overview of how you can build such a plan:

> - *Strategies.* Prepare a list of five things you do to market yourself or your law firm and rank those things in the order of what has worked best (for example, networking, seminars, Web site, advertising, and media relations). Then cross off the bottom two items and focus your time and resources on the top three.
>
> - *Clients.* Create a profile of your ideal client and develop a marketing strategy that focuses on this target, not on everyone. You can increase your revenue dramatically by focusing on the demographics, occupation, location, financials and other characteristics of clients who will give you the work that you want.
>
> - *Work.* Free up time for profitable new work by (1) declining matters from an existing client that are less profitable; or (2) increasing your fee to reinforce client perceptions that you're good and you're in demand by many people, which

allows you to command a high price for your
services—the definition of successful marketing.

- ► *Mix.* Make sure that no single client exceeds 10
  percent of your total revenue. Thus, if any one
  client "forgets" to pay you, or even leaves, the
  loss won't be so hard to handle. I have seen too
  many firms focus on a very few, larger clients
  and be severely damaged when the fees from
  that client fail to continue—from dissatisfaction,
  change of billing attorney, merger, recession, or
  other unanticipated problems.

Bankers know that new clients are the lifeblood of any business and that a scattershot marketing approach is counterproductive to securing new clients.

Section 5:

Establishing Your Creditworthiness

Once your bank understands your firm's viability as a business entity, it will want assurance that you are creditworthy as a customer. Banks extend credit to law firms based on the results of two general types of testing measures: One is quantitative and the other is qualitative. Let's review the quantitative measures first, which include your FICO credit score and the credit-reporting agencies' VantageScore.

The FICO credit score

The FICO credit score, which was created by Fair Isaac Corporation (a credit analysis firm), is the number that most bankers use to determine whether they want to lend money to someone. Essentially, the number is an estimate of the risk that you will default on a payment, generally within the first three years of a loan. The national median score is 720. The highest possible score is 850.

Your FICO score is based on your history of borrowing and repaying money. Therefore, knowing your score in advance of applying for a loan can make the process flow more smoothly. There are several sources for obtaining that information. Go to www.myfico.com (a division

What's in Your FICO® score?

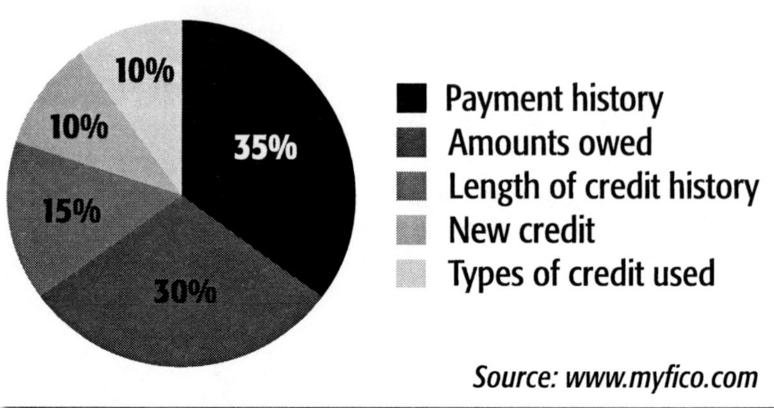

of Fair Issacs) to learn your options, as well as to get more details on the scoring system overall. Note that federal law gives you the right to get a free copy of your credit report—but not your FICO score—once every three months.

While the best assurance of securing a loan is always a strong relationship with your banker, there are practical steps you can take to improve your credit score, and to improve your banking relationship in the process. Key steps include the following:

- ▸ Pay all your bills on time.

- ▸ Don't use more than 50 percent of your credit limit on any one credit card, even if you pay monthly.

- ▸ Think twice about closing an account, even if you don't use it, since losing a line of credit increases your overall credit usage ratio.

- Use your accounts at least once a year.

- Remember that the older your average account is, the better your score will be.

- Don't apply for smaller credit cards or loans when you apply for a large loan within the same year.

- Maintain a diverse debt portfolio, as that is favored over having only credit cards.

- Three to five cards should be the most you have to reach the highest score.

Also, be aware that the Fair Credit Reporting Act amendment effective December 1, 2004, allows banks to report information about your accounts to credit bureaus, which makes good banking relations even more important.

The VantageScore

The three big national credit-reporting agencies that serve as the repositories of individual and commercial credit reports are Equifax, Experian, and TransUnion.

These three major credit-reporting firms have long used individual formulas to calculate credit scores, with varying grades a possible result. In March 2006, however, all three companies jointly announced that they would standardize how they calculate consumer credit scores. The goal was to make the numbers easier for lenders and borrowers to understand. The announcement essentially amounted to a competitive challenge to Fair Isaac's FICO system.

The big three's new joint scoring system, called "VantageScore," is intended to provide a more consistent credit scoring process. The companies will continue to separately collect data for credit files, which they sell to creditors and consumers. But individual credit scores from the three firms, say executives, should be the same if the companies' files on that individual contain the same data. The system will give scores ranging from 501 to 990, which in turn will translate to grades of "A" through "F." Consumers with scores above 900 will be A credit risks, those with scores above 800 but less than 901 will rate a B risk, and so on.

At this early date, it remains to be seen whether this new system will supplant the traditional FICO score. What is certain, though, is that under any scoring system, consistently paying bills on time, having a long history of paying different types of bills, and using credit modestly will result in a higher credit score.

Qualitative factors: The four Cs

Ultimately more important than quantitative score numbers are the qualitative factors that bankers use to gauge your creditworthiness. Collectively called the "Four Cs," these factors are your character, collateral, capacity (also known as cash flow), and capital. Bankers will seriously weight these factors in their decision-making processes.

Character. The first question a banker asks is whether the ethics, business practices, and general reputation of the prospective customer or borrower are such that

The Big Three Credit Agencies

- **Equifax:** P.O. Box 740241, Atlanta, GA 30374-0241; (800) 525-6285; www.econsumer.equifax.com

- **Experian:** P.O. Box 9532, Allen, TX 75013; (888) 397-3742; www.experian.com

- **TransUnion:** P.O. Box 6790, Fullerton, CA 92834-6790; (800) 680-7289; www.transunion.com

To obtain a free credit report once every 12 months from each of the nationwide credit-reporting companies, visit www.annualcreditreport.com (the central site set up by Equifax, Experian, and TransUnion).

the bank can feel comfortable—meaning, does the bank want to do business with this party? Without this threshold question being answered in the affirmative, there will be no further discussion. The elements of character are honesty, integrity, ability, and reputation in the community.

Capacity. The next question is whether the law firm's cash flow is sufficient to justify confidence that the loan-carrying costs (interest and related charges) and the loan's principal amount will be paid back at the appointed time. A cash-flow statement must be submitted for the bank's consideration. Calculating the ability to repay a loan is a process of identifying and deducting the practice's expenses from the monthly cash received. One method for estimating it is the turnover ratio, which is defined as:

Accounts receivable balance divided by the result of billings per days in the billing period (either monthly or annually)

The turnover ratio tells the banker that the lawyer can expect payment for billings x number of days after a

---

"A man's fortunes are the fruit of his character."

–Ralph Waldo Emerson

---

client receives a statement. The national average for law firms is between 120 and 150 days—as long as five months. The lesson: Cash flow and collections are the crucial determinants of business performance and, thus, of loan repayment ability.

Collateral. Even if the bank is careful in agreeing to provide a loan, the loan could still go into default. So if all else fails, how will the bank's outstanding loan be repaid? The "back door," as some bankers call it, is the value and adequacy of the collateral that was given to the bank to secure the debt's repayment in accordance with the terms of the loan. Collateral can be a "hard" asset such as a house, another piece of real estate, or equipment used in the operation of the law firm. Collateral can also be a personal guarantee by someone with adequate wealth to honor the guarantee if you default. It can include securities and a lien on accounts receivable as well.

Capital. The bank needs to know what the loan funds will be used for. Then, in turn, if the loan proceeds will be used to purchase an asset, the bank wants to know how much of that cost will be covered by the law firm's own assets—in other words, how much equity (or debt-to-equity ratio) the firm will have in the asset. Banks do not want to risk being the only party investing in the given asset; they want to know that the law firm has a substantial stake in the purchase, too. The banker wants the bank's risk to be limited to the analysis of the firm's ability to repay the loan, even if the ultimate purchase does not work out or does not produce the income expected. Accordingly, if the firm has an adequate capital base in the investment, the bank will be more comfortable helping complete the purchase.

As a side note, it has been said that law firms often need working capital loans. Technically, the advance of funds under a loan does not change the working capital. The more correct statement is that the loan is being made to help the law firm meet its liquidity or cash needs. The bank must be assured that there is sufficient equity in the law firm to repay the loan in accordance with the loan terms.

Section 6:

Obtaining a Commercial Loan

The literal payoff of demonstrating your good business sense and establishing your creditworthiness will take place when you need to ask your banker for a loan. Whether you're an established firm or a new and growing one, the fundamental reason for seeking a bank loan is that cash needs exceed the firm's ability to generate cash through client receipts and partner capital.

Reasons for seeking a loan

Your cash needs may reflect short-term or long-term considerations, and they could include the following factors.

Rapid growth. Faster growing firms need more cash to cover the costs of adding staff, equipment, and new office space. Expenses for these must be met at the time they are incurred, and your current receivables collection may not be enough to cover them. (As noted before, there is usually a time lag in the collection of accounts receivable, with the average for law firms running up to five months.)

Disaster recovery. If your firm has been hit by a fire or a natural disaster (which often is a question of when, not if), you will likely need an emergency loan to secure funds for rent, payroll, insurance settlements, new office arrangements, supplies, and much more.

Operating considerations. An unexpected tax liability, slower than anticipated receivables collection, or higher than anticipated operating expenses—any of these can require an immediate cash infusion to offset them.

Technology expenditures. Purchasing new computers and software, or even subscribing to an expanded database research service, can have a significant future return on investment. However, payment for these and other capital expenses must be made up front, at the time incurred.

Any of these situations would be sufficient to seek a bank loan in order to meet their initial costs.

Amount of the loan

A truly competent banker will be able to review your firm's performance and future prospects as set forth in your planning documents and advise you whether your loan request is for an appropriate amount or if it is too little. If the loan request is too small, a good banker will suggest that you request a higher loan advance.

Here is an example of what an effective banker can do. When I was in the food processing business, our company had had the same loan officer for many years. At one point, the officer was to retire so he introduced me to another loan officer in the bank who was to take charge of our account. The new loan

officer reviewed all the financial information and history of our company. In a subsequent meeting, he said to me, "You have been asking for far too little money in order to operate your business and grow effectively." I was shocked to hear a banker say to me, "You need to borrow more money from me." But he was right. We had been operating on a shoestring, believing that there was no way our limited collateral was sufficient to warrant a larger loan.

This banker taught me a very important lesson: A good banker will make it possible for you to grow your business within the parameters required by both the bank and the federal regulatory agencies. While in this particular case, my company did not obtain a larger amount of money, the banker adjusted the methodology of repaying the loan in such a way that the net effect of our borrowing tripled the impact on our business. Good bankers will understand your business and make sure that both you as the borrower and they as the lender collaborate to make your relationship as powerful as it can possibly be—to the benefit of *both* parties.

Types of loans

Banks often have set guidelines for the types of loans they extend to lawyers. The amount of the total loan package may be limited to a set amount, such as three times the monthly expenses excluding partner draws. Ask your banker what his or her constraints or parameters are.

These parameters typically define the loans granted by many lending institutions:

- *Revolving line of credit.* The lawyer borrows and repays at will up to the amount of the credit line. The bank usually prefers that the borrower be out of debt for at least 30 to 90 days each year. The line of credit is then reviewed annually and extended, increased, or terminated as circumstances warrant.

- *Line of credit.* The borrower obtains a designated sum of money over a period of time. The credit line is then converted to a term loan, repayable over a period of from two to five years.

- *Equipment term loan.* The amount of the loan to purchase new equipment will normally be no longer than the depreciable life of the equipment, usually three to five years.

▶ *Term loan.* These can be as long as seven to
ten years for a large law firm, three to five
for a smaller firm. Most involve leasehold
improvements and furniture and equipment
purchases. Frequently the term loan is drawn
down over a period of six to nine months, and
payback begins within three months of the final
draw. Payments may be all equal until the loan
is paid in full, or a larger "balloon" payment may
be required at the end of the loan term.

Negotiating the loan

When you're ready to request a loan, you need to set
up a meeting with your banker. By this time, your
banker should have all the essentials to evaluate
whether you will receive the loan. The essentials
include your credit score, "4 Cs" profile, business
plans, and business documentation. Just to be sure,
take copies of your plan summaries and important
documents with you to the meeting.

You should also prepare a one-page summary—
sometimes called an executive summary—stating
what you want to use the loan for and how you

intend to pay it back. Include all supporting financial information, and consider taking your accountant to the meeting, too. Be prepared to show proof of *and* answer any questions about the following:

- ▸ Whether your accounting is done on a cash basis (collections and expenses only, which is more common for small firms) or an accrual basis (which also includes work-in-progress and accounts receivable)

- ▸ What your current profit margin is and whether you are implementing any cost-containment strategies

- ▸ How much you have in working capital

- ▸ What your current receivables are and how they reflect your realization rates when expressed as (1) a percentage of booked hours billed and (2) a percentage of billed hours collected

- ▸ Where you stand on your utilization rate—i.e., the percentage of a workweek (usually expressed as an annual average) that you actually bill

- ▸ A listing of WIP by client, which will become accounts receivable at a future date

Make sure that you fully understand the time frame for approval and that you are clear about all fees involved (including filing fees and other charges). Always request a commitment letter for the loan that the bank agrees to give you. In general, it is a good idea to ask for more money than you actually need because your loan request can be received in one of four ways:

1. You get everything you ask for.

2. Your request is granted but for a lower amount than you asked for.

3. Your request is granted in full but at a higher interest rate than you expected.

4. Your loan application is rejected.

If you've established an effective banking relationship, the latter three eventualities are less likely. But if the second or third alternative occurs, you may have the opportunity to negotiate and compromise by accepting the lesser amount (which is easier to do if you have asked for more than you needed) in exchange for something such as a longer term or reduced interest rate.

The lending process should be the culmination of everything you have established at the bank and should validate your law firm's viability and future growth prospects.

A good banker will make it possible for you to grow your business within the parameters required by both the bank and the federal regulatory agencies.

Section 7:

Obtaining SBA Financing*

To facilitate commercial bank loans, smaller law firms should definitely consider engaging the assistance of the Small Business Administration (SBA). The SBA was created 50 years ago as a vehicle for programs designed to give small businesses greater access to capital. The SBA does not make direct loans itself. Instead, it provides loan guarantees that enable banks to create profitable relationships with growing businesses.

Under SBA lending programs, banks fund 100 percent of the loan and get the government's guarantee on repayment for stated portions of the loan. Financial institutions use this type of program when they can't take full risk but really like particular borrowers and want to work with them (a not uncommon dynamic between lawyers and bankers). This is a great program when there is a shortfall of collateral for a conventional loan, which can be typical for law firms,

---

* Information in this section was generously provided by Joanne Thompson, Managing Partner of SBA OneSource, LLC, 600 17th St., Suite 2800, South, Denver, CO 80202.

especially smaller ones. This section overviews the main elements of the SBA's lending programs. For comprehensive details, related forms and templates, and ongoing news on SBA programs, go to www.sba.gov.

Types of SBA loan programs

Three types of SBA loan programs are of most direct application to law firms:

- ▸ The SBA 7a loan program, which can be either in the form of a term loan or a line of credit (the latter sometimes called SBA Express)

- ▸ The SBA 504 loan program, which concentrates on financing for purchases of real estate or capital equipment

- ▸ The CAPline program, which encompasses asset-based revolving loans

7a loan program. The 7a term loan program provides for a maximum loan guarantee of $1.5 million. For loans of less than $150,000, up to 85 percent can be guaranteed, with a guarantee fee equal to 2 percent of the guarantee portion of the loan. Loans of more than $150,000 can be guaranteed up to 75 percent, with a guarantee fee ranging from 3 percent to as high as 3.75 percent (for loans of over $1 million). The term loan/revolving line of credit feature of this program, *SBA Express,* provides loans of up to $350,000 through approved banks, with a 50 percent guarantee and interest rates (fixed or floating) that range as high as prime plus 6.5 percent. The "express" tag refers to the

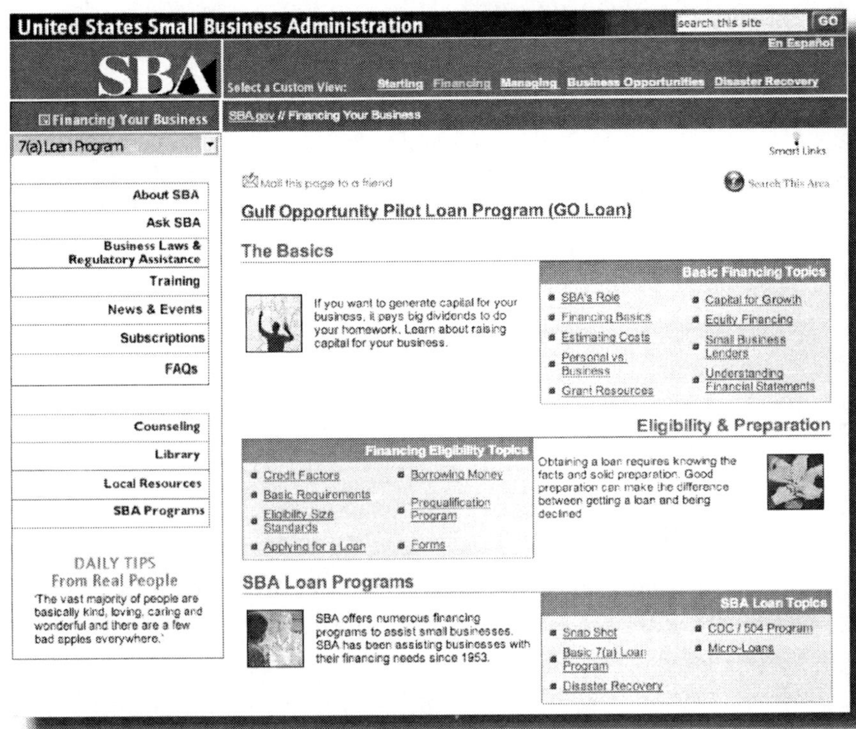

The SBA's Web site offers a host of information relating to its lending programs.

fact that applications receive a three-day turnaround from the SBA.

504 loan program. This program provides long-term, fixed-rate financing that enables small businesses to acquire real estate or capital equipment. The maximum loan amount can be as high as $4 million, but it more typically maxes out at $1.5 million. For a typical loan, the usual division is 50 percent for the bank (which gets first deed of trust), 40 percent for the SBA, and 10 percent for the borrower.

CAPline program. CAPline involves asset-based revolving loans that most typically are used to meet seasonal demands, such as those facing contractors and builders. However, law firms that have seasonal business peaks (for example, tax law specialists) might consider this option. Most 7a loan features apply, with a maximum guarantee amount of $1.5 million and a percentage of 75 percent.

Eligibility and proceeds use

SBA requirements for loan eligibility and proceeds use are generally a matter of common sense. Eligible businesses must be for-profit, must have reasonable owner equity to invest, and must be "small" according to SBA definitions by type of industry category. For law firms and other professional services businesses, the criterion is $6.5 million or less in annual revenues.

The loan proceeds can be used to fund real estate purchases, new construction, capital equipment and furniture purchases, or start-up expenses. In addition, SBA loans can be used to refinance other loans deemed to have been made on "unreasonable terms." Simply trying to obtain a lower interest rate is typically not a valid purpose for an SBA loan, but refinancing business credit card purchases generally qualifies.

Maturity and interest rates

The maturity of SBA-guaranteed loans varies based on how the proceeds are being used. Loans for working capital and business acquisitions cannot exceed 10 years. Although equipment loans are usually for a maximum of 10 years, they are limited to the economic life of the equipment being financed. Real estate loans cannot exceed a 25-year maximum.

In addition, loans can be "blended"—for example, certain portions each going to purchase durable equipment and provide working capital—with maturity determined by a weighting formula.

The interest rates may be fixed or variable, depending on loan amount and maturity, and are equal to the prime rate plus a certain percentage. Typically, the larger the loan and the shorter the maturity, the smaller the interest rate will be. For example, a loan of more than $50,000 for less than seven years could be at prime plus 2.25 percent, while a loan of less than $25,000 for more than seven years could be at prime plus 4.75 percent.

Requirements and responsibilities

Anyone owning 20 percent or more of the borrowing entity must personally guarantee an SBA loan. This is an unlimited guarantee. Such a borrower must pledge collateral (real estate or financial assets) to the extent that the loan is fully collateralized on a liquidation value basis. However, the SBA will not decline a loan where the sole weakness is a shortfall of collateral.

There is also a personal liquidity test, in which each owner of 20 percent or more of the business must contribute to the borrowing entity "excess" personal liquid assets (cash or savings) of one to two times the loan, depending on the amount. The borrower also pays a guarantee fee ranging from 2 percent of loans under $150,000 to 3.75 percent of loans for more than $1 million.

Lastly, the borrower is responsible for loan processing fees and prepayment penalties that vary by type of loan.

"It has been said that the love of money is the root of all evil. The want of money is so quite as truly."

—Samuel Butler

Section 8:
Managing Your Cash Flow

A cash-flow statement can have multiple names: a cash-flow budget, a statement of cash, or a forecast. But whatever moniker you give it, this statement is *the* single most important tool for the success of any business. Given that fact, you should be sure to review your cash-flow statement on at least a weekly, if not a daily, basis.

Effective cash flow management often comes down to the steps taken to get funds into the bank account as quickly as possible. Often these are commonsense efficiencies in dealing with your money that, over time, can make a tremendous difference to your "bottom line" and, correspondingly, to your creditworthiness in the eyes of your banker. Let's consider the commonsense steps that every law practice should implement.

Deposit revenue immediately upon receipt and spread the payment of bills throughout the month. If you pay bills all at once, it will cause an exaggerated drop in your bank balance.

Deposits

Do not wait to deposit checks. This is the first rule of cash flow management. While a check is being held for deposit, too many catastrophic events can occur. For one, the client may become angry and stop payment, or may have insufficient funds when the check is finally presented for clearance, or may become party to a lawsuit or other proceeding in which financial assets are attached. Deposit all checks even if the amount paid does not match what you billed. The variance can be negotiated or corrected later.

Another primary rule is maintaining a high average daily balance. Many banks calculate this figure as part of account statements, and it is one of the important factors they consider when asked to make a loan. You thus want to maintain as high a balance as possible, either by keeping a large sum of money in the bank or by keeping limited funds in the account for a longer period of time. Do this by depositing revenue immediately upon receipt and spreading the payment of bills throughout the month. If you pay bills all at once, it will cause an exaggerated drop in your bank balance.

Access to funds

Negotiate for immediate access to deposits. Some banks will place a "hold" on funds deposited with them until the funds have cleared through the banking system. This may be as long as seven days. Deposited "drafts" will take even longer to clear. However, you can negotiate with a bank over the timing of access to your deposited funds, so speak to your banker about it.

Analyze the "availability of funds" schedule at your bank, which is required by law to make the schedule available. Depending on your bank's policy, you may not be able to draw out cash against checks in your deposit for several days. Determine the number of days your bank will restrict your use of the funds in your deposits.

Administration

A top efficiency in administering your accounts is reconciling your bank statements immediately upon receipt. The immediate correction of errors, whether made by your bank or you, is critical.

"Take care of the pence, and the pounds will take care of themselves."

—Proverb

In addition, consider an automatic bank sweep. Banks provide for an "automatic sweep" on a daily basis. Establish a minimum amount of money, such as $2,500, to remain in your general account. The exact sum will depend on the amount of checks and deposits that pass through your bank account each month. Then, instruct the bank to segregate all funds in excess of this amount at the end of each day and "sweep" or transfer those "excess" funds into a money market (interest-bearing) account until they're needed. The bank can also be instructed to call you, or to automatically transfer funds into the general account from the money market account, in the event the balance goes below the established minimum amount.

Another important step is to maintain separate payroll and general accounts, placing in the payroll account the full amount of gross payroll (including employee portion of taxes) on the day that payroll is due. It is never a good idea to use payroll money to operate the firm. Employers have been known to "borrow" payroll and payroll tax funds in the hope that enough accounts receivable will be collected in a day or two

to cover the shortfall. (Oh, the eternal optimist!)
However, if they fail to receive the funds expected and
cannot cover payroll and taxes sufficiently, the result
will be civil and potential criminal penalties. The
general account should be maintained only with those
funds necessary to cover the normal flow of checks
that are presented to the bank that day for collection,
in accord with the preceding "sweep" discussion.

Also make sure you get full credit for balances
maintained in all accounts. For example, one account
may not keep enough balances to offset fees, while the
other account may keep an excess.

Lastly, negotiate for a lockbox with the bank. Many
banks advertise this as one of their premier business
services. In this arrangement, the bank picks up
remittances several times a day, records them, and
sends details of the transaction to you as the customer
within several days. Modern technology now allows
communicating this information on the same day the
deposit is made, or on the day following the deposit.
This saves the time of opening the mail and processing
the deposit. If a lockbox is not cost-effective, be sure
that remittances that are received are deposited with
the bank on the same day—which is an absolute rule.

Section 9:

Managing the Merchant Banking Relationship

Having a merchant account—an account that is deemed to be a business account—can be important in handling your practice's finances effectively. Such accounts normally allow the lawyer to get access to funds more quickly and more easily.

General accounts versus trust accounts

Your engagement agreement with a client will control how and when you get paid, in that the agreement of the parties normally controls (except for unconscionable or unreasonable charges) the relationship between client and lawyer. Whether fees charged and paid should be deposited into the client's trust account or the lawyer's general account is not pertinent to this discussion. Suffice it to say that payment for work *already* performed is generally to be deposited into a general account, and payment for work *to be* performed is generally to be deposited into a client's trust account.

All your engagement agreements should set forth in detail the circumstances under which funds may or must be transferred from the client's trust account to the lawyer's general account. When the lawyer is entitled to make the transfer, the lawyer *must* make the transfer or be guilty of commingling his or her personal funds with the client's funds—a "no-no" under the rules of professional conduct.

Caveats about credit cards

An increasing number of law firms now accept client payments by credit card for services rendered. If you arrange with your bank to accept credit card payments, be aware of the following essential caveats:

- ▸ Client payments by credit card should only be

for legal services rendered. They should not be requested or accepted for unearned retainers or charge-backs of unearned fees. (An exception *might* occur when a separate account is set up and all bank charges and credit card company charges are immediately paid for out of the lawyer's general account.)

▸ Arrange with the client that any dispute over fees paid by card will not be raised with or adjudicated by the credit card company. In other words, the client agrees that the charge is nonrefundable. The credit card company, when shown the client's agreement, will not credit the client or debit the law firm in the event of a future dispute. The proper forum for adjudicating the dispute thus remains with the state bar disciplinary system and the courts. The client can agree to binding arbitration. So, too,

the client can agree not to use the credit card company for leverage in a fee dispute.

- ▸ Do not charge clients for credit card processing fees. The processing charge is overhead, just like lights and rent. Unfortunately, too many lawyers still think of expense items as profit centers. Clients increasingly resent such charges and will no longer permit or accept them. When effort is still made to assess such charges, clients generally will refuse to pay by credit card. This will result in delays in payment to the lawyer. In addition, your contract with your credit card company and merchant account organization may prohibit surcharges and subject you to penalties if you try to assess them.

Now let's look at trust accounts in more detail in the next section.

Do not charge clients for credit card processing fees. The processing charge is overhead, just like lights and rent.

Section 10:

Using Trust Accounts Effectively

Disciplinary rule requirements

The American Bar Association's Model Code of Professional Responsibility specifically addresses the issue of trust accounts and commingling of funds. Disciplinary Rule DR 9-102, "Preserving Identity of Funds and Property of a Client," states the following:

(A) All funds of clients paid to a lawyer or law firm, other than advances for costs and expenses, shall be deposited in one or more identifiable bank accounts maintained in the state in which the law office is situated and no funds belonging to the lawyer or law firm shall be deposited therein except as follows:

(1) Funds reasonably sufficient to pay bank charges may be deposited therein.

(2) Funds belonging in part to a client and in part presently or potentially to the lawyer or law firm must be deposited therein, but the

portion belonging to the lawyer or law firm may be withdrawn when due unless the right of the lawyer or law firm to receive it is disputed by the client, in which event the disputed portion shall not be withdrawn until the dispute is finally resolved.

The conclusion to be drawn from this requirement is that money earned by a lawyer for provision of services belongs to the lawyer and must be removed from the client's trust account when earned. This must be done immediately (unless jurisdictional rules state otherwise), with the earned money being placed in the lawyer's general account.

So when you first receive funds, the question to be answered is which account should they be placed into—the trust account or the general account? Use the following as a rule of thumb:

- If the funds are provided on retainer, then they are for a task that is not completed and the hours are not yet earned, which means the money goes into the client trust account.

- If the funds have been earned when you receive them, then they should go into the general account.

Note that some jurisdictions may place additional requirements on the withdrawal of funds from a trust account. In Wisconsin, as one example, the requirement is that before any funds can be withdrawn from the client trust account, the client must be given five days' notice. This is so even when the funds are earned and even if the engagement

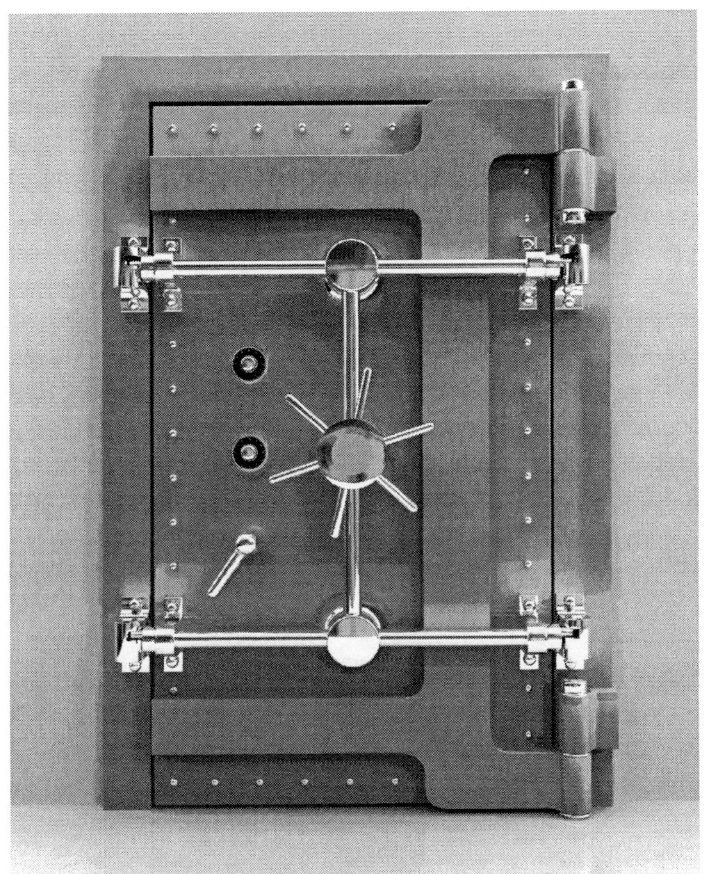

agreement provides for immediate withdrawal. Thus, as always, it's important to verify the rules in your jurisdiction before making an immediate withdrawal of earned funds.

Flat, retained, and split fees

If you charge a flat fee and agree that it is earned upon receipt, withdrawal must be made. It may, though, be better to deposit the flat fee into a client's trust account and withdraw when reaching specific events that qualify as services for which fees are earned, such as the filing of a complaint or signing of a settlement or merger agreement.

Even retainer fees can be deposited into a general account if the agreement says that the retainer is not for future work but is, instead, for the lawyer specifically being engaged (and thus taken off the market). In other words, there is a valid charge for not being available to others. Opinions on the subject suggest that the retainer for this purpose must be "reasonable," as negotiated and detailed in the engagement agreement. If you receive a retainer for future work, it would seem best to put this into your client's trust account. However, it is again best that the engagement agreement provide for this upon realizing a certain date or event.

When discussing flat or fixed fees, the hours involved are irrelevant. If you compute the flat fee based on the number of hours you anticipate and discuss this with the client (suggesting that the fee will increase if actual hours exceed the estimate), that looks like hourly billing.

Some lawyers will split the type of fee that's charged, making part of it a nonrefundable retainer and placing the balance into the trust account for withdrawal as the work is performed. This method may be preferable because it makes a clear distinction between the two elements—one nonrefundable and one to be paid only when it is earned or the work is actually performed. Even with the latter method, however, you should specify the event or date that

Rule of Thumb for Where to Deposit Funds

- ▸ If the funds are provided on retainer, then they are for a task that is not completed and the hours are not yet earned, which means the money goes into the client trust account.

- ▸ If the funds have been earned when received, then they go into the general account.

triggers allowing you to take money from the trust account and placing it into the general account. This avoids your having to wait for the client to say "yes" on the funds after the fact and, therefore, allows you to have the money sooner.

Trust account access

All lawyers should specify in their engagement letters that the client authorizes the lawyer to debit IOLTA trust account funds after a reasonable time from the date of billing—for example, 15, 30, or 45 days, whichever is most reasonable under the circumstances. This provides a date certain for payment to the lawyer. In most jurisdictions, of course, the client will retain the right to dispute the charges, although clients are unlikely to do so if they understand that, by agreement, they need to be timely with any objections. The real issue, however, is that when the fee is earned, it must be withdrawn from the client's trust account. Otherwise, it's commingling—which violates the code.

Commingling is a major potential problem. Generally bar associations have taken the attitude that even $100 of personal funds in a client's trust account is commingling of the lawyer's and client's funds. Today most banks do not require a deposit of your own funds to open a trust account, so resist any request to do so. This issue requires discussion and perhaps negotiation with your bank. Further, you should look to any relevant "treaty" that may exist between your state's bar and banking associations.

In addition, it is important to lay out a "protest process" in your engagement agreement. Provide that if you don't receive a complaint or dispute in writing from the client within the number of days from the date of the invoice or statement set forth in the agreement, the client will be deemed to have approved the billing. If the client protests later, you will have a *prima facie* reason for the transfer and the money will be in your pocket (not the trust account), except as otherwise provided in your jurisdiction's rules of professional conduct.

The importance of trust accounts

Clearly, trust accounts are very important to the lawyer, but it should be emphasized that these accounts are also very important, and desirable, to the bank where they are deposited. Client trust funds can offer a large and stable deposit for the bank, although it depends on the nature of the law practice. A criminal law practice, for example, might not involve large trust deposits, but a substantial personal injury, family law, or real estate practice would.

Clients' trust account money tends to stay in the account for a period of time longer than in the lawyer's general account—and with reason, because general account funds are used for operating expenses. Trust account funds thus bolster the financial assets against which a bank makes loans, allowing it to loan more money in accord with standard banking ratios of deposits to loans. And, of course, loans and not deposits are a bank's source of income.

All of this is to say that trust accounts can be a considerable source of leverage for a law firm in negotiating fees and services with a bank. Because these accounts increase the bank's ability to make profitable loans, you might ask your bank for additional services at no charge (such as no-cost checking accounts or financial management services for staff members) in exchange for maintaining a minimum trust account balance. As stated elsewhere in this report, lawyers are desirable banking customers for many reasons—and recognizing that fact by negotiating mutually advantageous terms can only help both parties in the business relationship.

Section 11:

Using Other Bank Services

A good bank will provide lawyers with the services and the responsiveness they want. An effective bank can handle more than essential financial transactions involving loans and cash management. It can also handle a wide range of other services that make law firms more efficient businesses and help lawyers manage their personal finances. This section gives an overview of some primary points.

Services for law firms

Credit card services. If you have the client's credit card information and permission to charge his or her account, you will get paid more readily and it improves cash flow. The few dollars it costs you to get the money faster—typically 2 percent to 4 percent, depending on your volume, the card, and your ability to negotiate with your bank and processing agent—is offset by the ease and assurance of payment, as well as the speed of collection.

Office services. Many banks offer services relating to functions such as staff payroll and pension administration, and even monthly billing and collection.

Investment instruments. Law firms can earn a return on cash balances not needed for operating purposes by placing the money into such short-term investment instruments as certificates of deposit, business money market accounts, commercial paper, or U.S. government obligations—all of which a bank can provide.

Online financial services. These services can facilitate your cash management. For example, banks offer the opportunity to set minimum and maximum cash balances in a firm's general account, with "extra" funds being transferred daily into interest-bearing accounts and cash advances being drawn from a line of credit if the general account falls below the minimum.

Deposit considerations for lawyers

For the most part, lawyers still get paid by personal checks from clients and must physically deposit the checks with the bank. While the check-deposit transaction can involve special considerations relating to lawyers, establishing a sound cash deposit relationship with your bank can help you to manage them.

For example, an attorney is not automatically authorized to endorse the client's name to checks. Unfortunately, too many disciplinary cases involve lawyers forging endorsements to settlement checks, or lying to the client about whether the check was received, and then walking off with the proceeds. This can be an issue with a two-party check in which one of the parties is not available to endorse it (for example, because the party is out of the country).

Banks can refuse any deposit for any reason, so the trick here is to negotiate the check against your account. In other words, cash the check first. By accepting the two-party check as a deposit, banks may feel they would have liability if there was a dispute between the parties. A bank that is a member of the Federal Reserve System must negotiate a check for you. But by cashing rather than depositing the check, the liability for any dispute is on the account holder, and the bank believes it does not assume liability. As long as you have the funds in your account to cover the check, it should go through.

There are, however, two caveats relating to this:

- First, your funds equivalent to the amount of the check will be placed on hold until the check clears. This won't be a problem if you turn around and deposit the funds to the account. Any hold can only be until the check actually clears, which is usually midnight the same day according to the newest check-clearing rules, although some banks will hold checks for more than $5,000 slightly longer.

- Second, if the check is refused by the originating bank or is disputed elsewhere, you are liable to make your bank whole.

Banks can refuse any deposit for any reason, so the trick here is to negotiate the check against your account.

Plus, there is a final check-deposit consideration that affects all banking customers. The USA Patriot Act requires financial institutions to take extra security precautions that help the government fight the funding of terrorism and money-laundering activities. Federal law requires all financial institutions to obtain, verify, and record information that identifies each person who opens an account. This would not ordinarily be a problem, except that there have been reports of some banks using the Patriot Act as an excuse to refuse deposit of checks made out in ways other than the exact name of the checking account (for example, refusing deposit of a check made out to "John Smith Law Offices" when the name of the account is "The Law Offices of John Smith").

You can avoid this problem with the multiple ways people make out checks by creating an endorsement stamp that reads, "Pay to the Order of The Law Offices of John Smith, For Deposit Only," and that also includes the bank name and account number.

Personal banking services

Last but not least, the banking services that are offered to any consumer represent an opportunity to a lawyer whose firm has established a good banking relationship. That business relationship can often be used to give you greater access to *and* more effective pricing for such personal banking services as these:

- ▸ Personal loans

- ▸ Home mortgages

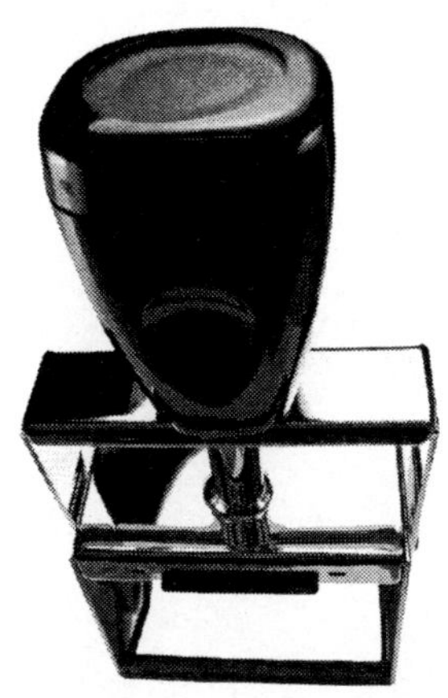

An easy way to avoid several problems is to use an endorsement stamp on checks. Be sure to include:

- **"For Deposit Only"**

- **Your firm name**

- **Your bank account number**

- Discount brokerage services

- Trust and estate services

- Personal financial planning

- Retirement counseling

- Discounts on standard banking services for your staff, such as lower-cost auto loans or no-fee checking accounts.

As your needs develop and change over time, be sure to talk to your banker about the various types of assistance the institution can provide to you.

Section 12:

Strengthening the Lawyer-Banker Relationship

As with any relationship (be it a business one or otherwise), having a strong lawyer-banker relationship means you need to pay attention and invest a little effort to maintain the kind of ties that bind over the long term. Here are some final pointers to help you on that road.

Educating personnel

The relationship between lawyer and banker needs to be open and candid and built on trust. Good bankers are creative people who will find ways to assist their good customers. But bankers can be even more creative if they understand the lawyer's goals and business, which requires you to maintain an ongoing process of education with your banker. Over time, the banker can become a valuable source of information, advice, and new business referrals.

To grow the relationship from the outset, you should make your bank deposits personally until you get to know the bank personnel. Continue efforts to meet with the branch manager, the operations personnel, and the loan committee—the people

who can help you most. Only when you are on good terms with your bank's personnel should you either bank by mail or allow someone else in your office to make deposits for you.

Negotiating fees

Cash management and administrative services come at a price. Many firms don't realize that banks can be flexible on pricing and will add more services at the right price if your business relationship with them justifies it. Note, however, that if a bank focuses on doing business with lawyers, it will have less pricing flexibility because it will want to treat all lawyer-customers equally—you won't receive a price break that the bank does not extend to others.

You, the lawyer, must know what you value most. A bank that knows the legal industry will give you

sophistication plus higher prices. A bank seeking to break into the industry may know less but have more price flexibility.

Investigating alternatives

Even if you have a longstanding relationship with your bank, it doesn't hurt to investigate the competitive landscape. To find out what other banks are doing, talk to other lawyers, look at Bankrate.com or other resources available to law firms, or have a beauty contest in which you ask other banks to give you a proposal for services. Two things are essential in this process:

1. Make sure you compare the same or equivalent banking services.

2. Make sure there are no hidden charges for those services.

However, even if you learn that your current bank charges more for services than some of its competitors, it doesn't mean automatically that you should switch banks. Take a look at the relationship you've built over time. If another bank has submitted a lower bid for services, talk to your current bank, share the bids you received, say you value the existing relationship, and ask what the bank can do to maintain it.

Just as you would want your clients to handle a competitive bid situation in this way, it behooves you to do it with and for your bank.

Bankers can be even more creative if they understand the lawyer's goals and business, which requires you to maintain an ongoing process of education with your banker.

Section 13:

Learning from Experience

While megafirms will always find that banks are eager for their business, small firms and solo practitioners—which together make up the majority of the legal community—may find it harder to establish effective banking relationships. But it can be done, with banks large and small. How does it ultimately work? To illustrate, let's turn to some real-world tales.

The following anecdotes are culled from postings made by participants in a listserv oriented to small firms and solos, all responding to the question: "What do you like and dislike about your bank?" In these responses, which come from across the United States, you will find that lawyers can experience more than a few problems, particularly with local branches of large multinational banks. But you'll also see plenty of proof that bankers *do* appreciate their lawyer-clients—and that they can show it creatively.

"I've tried working with two large national banks that felt I wasn't worth the bother. So I went **over to my friendly credit union and they signed me up in a heartbeat.** They're open seven days a week, until 8:00 p.m. during the week. I have five personal and law firm accounts with them. They even notarize documents for free."

—From a Mid-Atlantic state capital

"For my IOLTA and operating accounts I use a money center bank that is 'professional-friendly,' having set up special programs for lawyers, accountants, and others offering free checks, online banking, and other services. They offer good interest rates on the IOLTA accounts, so you feel as though everybody is winning when you have money there. In a way, the **bank's attitude and service is a reflection of how I want my own firm perceived.** They care about their customers' individual needs, make things as easy and convenient as possible, deliver what they promise, and do a good job. That's what all clients and customers deserve."

—From Chicago

"I used a local bank that was great, but it has been progressively bought out and **none of the successors have good services.** If I tried to go back to a smaller bank, it ended up sold. I gave up on one bank after I went there three times and no one could figure out how to open a trust account."

—**From the Pacific Northwest**

"My bank has a name—Heather. She started out as a business banking associate and is now the assistant bank manager. When I wanted to open my business account, there she was ready to help. She **introduced me to other people in the branch, which led to some great networking** groups, and she keeps a stack of my cards on her desk for people who have legal questions or need estate planning. Next month my business will be 'spotlighted' at a table near the teller line for a week. It's a program they have for their small business customers, and it's how I found my accountant."

—From a Southeastern city

"I think the problem with banking today is that there is no 'face' on the bank. In the days of community-based banks, the local attorney knew all the bankers and could make a phone call on behalf of a client to ensure the granting of a loan. There was a high degree of mutual trust and support of the local banking community. Then the mergers started. Now, **it's like the bank-of-the-month club.** Worse yet, they transfer bank officers so often that it's hard to build a relationship."

—From a Western city

"A major regional bank recently opened two new branches near my office. A couple of months before opening my firm, I went in and met with the manager, who was more than happy to meet with me. She introduced me to a senior new accounts rep who was extraordinarily helpful. She answered all of my questions and, best of all, promised there would be no service charges for my accounts. Fast-forward to a few weeks before the 'grand opening,' when I finally had a need to actually open the accounts. I called the account rep, who immediately remembered me. I set a Saturday appointment to do the paperwork for the accounts. When I arrived, **both the manager and the account rep greeted me by name** and offered me coffee. The paperwork for the accounts was ready to go. The account rep told me she was *going out on maternity leave, and she called over the manager, who told me to call her directly if I had any questions on my accounts. They also gave me the name of another account rep who would be available to assist me.* ***I came away from that experience thinking I couldn't be happier."***

—From a major Eastern city

As you can see from these lawyers' individual experiences, the nature and effectiveness of the lawyer-banker relationship can vary. If, however, you invest the time required to choose a bank that's right for you and then build a solid relationship with your banker, you are far more likely to reap the many benefits that a good lawyer-banker relationship will bring.

Section 14:
Resources for Finding Out More

Banking

There are a variety of Internet resources that provide information on establishing a banking relationship and on comparative differences between banks and bank services. One of the most useful is Bankrate, Inc., www.bankrate.com. It's the Web's leading aggregator of financial rate information, with surveys of rates from approximately 4,800 financial institutions in all 50 states. This site provides free rate information on more than 300 financial products, including mortgages, credit cards, new and used automobile loans, money market accounts, certificates of deposit, checking and ATM fees, home equity loans, and online banking fees.

In addition, the American Bankers Association's Web site, www.aba.com, offers a variety of information resources to small businesses, including guidelines on how to analyze a financial statement, a glossary of banking terminology, and banking and the law. The association's flagship publication, the

ABA Banking Journal, is also online—at www.abaj.
com—and is a good source of information on current
industry trends.

General business

There are numerous resources for law firms that want
to better understand the role of banking in the general
context of business management. General resources
within the profession include the many programs,
publications, and materials of the American Bar
Association, www.aba.net. Plus, there are the
comprehensive online education programs found at
the West LegalEdCenter, www.westlegaled.com, which
compiles business and legal education programs from
the Practicing Law Institute, National Bar Association,
and many others.

General training programs and materials on
business literacy are available through the American
Management Association, www.amanet.org, The
Conference Board, www.conference-board.org, and
the Professional Services Management Association,
www.psmanet.org.

LawBiz® Management Company

The LawBiz® Management Company of Edward Poll
& Associates, Inc., at www.lawbiz.com, is a leading
consultant organization that works with lawyers
to increase their profits and their effectiveness at
practicing law. Edward Poll, J.D., M.B.A., CMC, the
author of this special report, is a nationally recognized

coach and adviser who gives coaching and strategic guidance to national and regional law firms and their leaders on practice management, business development, and financial matters. He has practiced law for 25 years, was the CEO and COO of several manufacturing businesses, and has been a business and profitability consultant to law firms for more than 15 years. He frequently writes and speaks on The Business of Law®, and his widely praised books— all available through his Web site, www.lawbiz. com—include the following titles (each published by LawBiz® unless otherwise noted):

- *Attorney and Law Firm Guide to the Business of Law: Planning and Operating for Survival and Growth,* Second Edition (American Bar Association, 2002). A comprehensive guide to all aspects of operating a law firm.

- *Collecting Your Fee: Getting Paid from Intake to Invoice* (American Bar Association, 2003). Advice on engagement letters, detailed bills, fee agreements, and intake forms.

- *The Best of Law Practice Management Review: The Audio Magazine for Busy Attorneys*™. One-hour audiotapes presenting expert interviews on the latest law practice management techniques.

- *The Profitable Law Office Handbook: Attorney's Guide to Successful Business Planning.* A best-selling practical guide that enables attorneys to take control of their financial futures.

- *Secrets of the Business of Law®: Successful Practices for Increasing Your Profits.* Specific suggestions for greater operating efficiency and profitable revenue generation.

► *MORE Secrets of the Business of Law®: Ways to Be More Effective, Efficient, and Profitable.* New hands-on tips and tactics for successful practice management, client relations, and much more.

"Keep thy shop, and thy shop will keep thee."

—Benjamin Franklin

Get these other informative books by Ed Poll

Attorney and Law Firm Guide to The Business of Law:
Planning and Operating for Survival and Growth
Second Edition
By Edward Poll

Do you want to:
* Be more successful by design than by accident?
* Be more profitable?
* Attract more clients?
* Have your clients pay on time?
* Have greater control of your practice?
* Have greater peace of mind?

If your answer is yes to any one of these questions, you must read this book. Ed Poll had simplified the mystical process of operating a law practice so anyone can be more effective with his or her clients and become more profitable.

Selling Your Law Practice:
The Profitable Exit Strategy
By Edward Poll

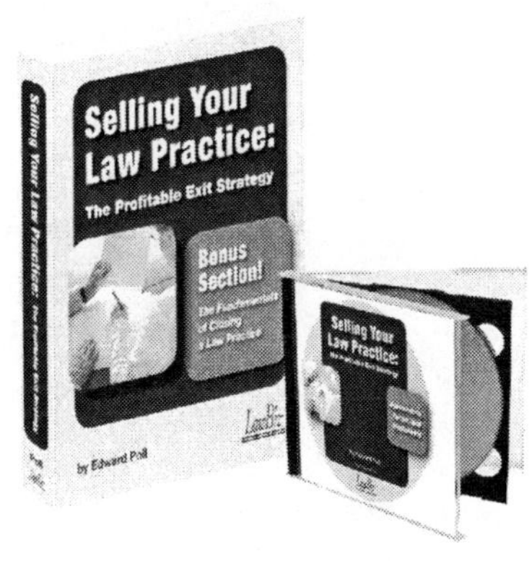

Get Top Dollar for Your Law Practice!

You will discover how to:
* Determine the value of your practice
* Set your sale price
* Evaluate and describe your practice's unique characteristics
* Negotiate the sale more effectively
* Anticipate transition issues
* Review state's Rules of Professional Conduct for selling a practice

The CD contains the sample contracts, forms, and financial worksheets from the book in Word and Excel format!

Call (800) 837-5880 or visit www.lawbiz.com to order!